50 Meals Under $10
Recipes for Home

By: Kelly Johnson

Table of Contents

- Spaghetti Aglio e Olio
- Vegetable Stir-Fry with Rice
- Bean and Cheese Quesadillas
- Tuna Salad Sandwiches
- Lentil Soup
- Veggie Fried Rice
- Baked Potato with Beans and Cheese
- Pasta Primavera
- Black Bean Tacos
- Tomato and Basil Bruschetta
- Chickpea Curry with Rice
- Greek Salad with Pita Bread
- Egg Fried Rice
- Vegetable Frittata
- Black Bean Soup
- Margherita Pizza
- Caprese Salad
- Spinach and Feta Quesadillas
- Tomato Soup with Grilled Cheese Sandwiches
- Mushroom Risotto
- Potato and Pea Samosas
- Vegetarian Chili
- Falafel with Hummus and Pita
- Cheese and Spinach Stuffed Shells
- Veggie Omelette with Toast
- Broccoli Cheddar Soup
- Rice and Bean Burritos
- Minestrone Soup
- Mushroom and Spinach Pasta
- Baked Beans on Toast
- Mexican Rice Casserole
- Sweet Potato and Black Bean Enchiladas
- Ratatouille
- Broccoli and Cheddar Quesadillas
- Peanut Noodles

- Lentil Tacos
- Tomato and Mozzarella Panini
- Creamy Mushroom Pasta
- Corn and Black Bean Salad
- Eggplant Parmesan
- Veggie Pad Thai
- BBQ Chickpea Wraps
- Spinach and Ricotta Stuffed Shells
- Black Bean and Corn Quesadillas
- Veggie Lo Mein
- Potato and Chickpea Curry
- Greek Quinoa Salad
- Spinach and Mushroom Quiche
- Veggie Fajitas
- Spicy Peanut Butter Noodles

Spaghetti Aglio e Olio

Ingredients:

- 8 ounces spaghetti
- 4 cloves garlic, thinly sliced
- 1/4 cup extra virgin olive oil
- 1/2 teaspoon red pepper flakes (adjust to taste)
- Salt, to taste
- Freshly ground black pepper, to taste
- Fresh parsley, chopped, for garnish
- Grated Parmesan cheese, for serving (optional)

Instructions:

1. Cook the spaghetti according to the package instructions until al dente. Reserve about 1/2 cup of pasta water before draining.
2. While the spaghetti is cooking, heat the olive oil in a large skillet over medium heat. Add the sliced garlic and red pepper flakes. Cook, stirring frequently, until the garlic is golden but not browned, about 1-2 minutes. Be careful not to burn the garlic.
3. Once the spaghetti is cooked, add it to the skillet with the garlic and oil. Toss to coat the spaghetti evenly with the oil.
4. If the pasta seems dry, add some of the reserved pasta water, a little at a time, until the spaghetti is lightly coated and glossy.
5. Season with salt and freshly ground black pepper to taste.
6. Serve hot, garnished with chopped parsley and grated Parmesan cheese, if desired.

Enjoy your Spaghetti Aglio e Olio! It's a simple yet delicious dish that's perfect for a quick and satisfying meal.

Vegetable Stir-Fry with Rice

Ingredients:

For the Stir-Fry:

- 2 cups mixed vegetables (such as bell peppers, broccoli, carrots, snap peas, mushrooms, etc.), sliced or chopped
- 2 tablespoons vegetable oil
- 2 cloves garlic, minced
- 1 teaspoon ginger, grated
- Salt and pepper, to taste
- Soy sauce or tamari, to taste (optional)

For the Rice:

- 1 cup uncooked rice (white or brown)
- 2 cups water or vegetable broth
- Pinch of salt

Instructions:

1. Start by cooking the rice. Rinse the rice under cold water until the water runs clear. In a saucepan, combine the rice, water or vegetable broth, and a pinch of salt. Bring to a boil, then reduce the heat to low, cover, and simmer for about 15-20 minutes (for white rice) or 40-45 minutes (for brown rice), or until the rice is tender and all the liquid is absorbed. Once done, remove from heat and let it sit covered for 5 minutes before fluffing with a fork.
2. While the rice is cooking, prepare the stir-fry. Heat the vegetable oil in a large skillet or wok over medium-high heat. Add the minced garlic and grated ginger, and sauté for about 30 seconds until fragrant.
3. Add the mixed vegetables to the skillet. Stir-fry for 4-5 minutes, or until the vegetables are tender-crisp and slightly caramelized.
4. Season the vegetables with salt and pepper to taste. If desired, you can also add a splash of soy sauce or tamari for extra flavor.
5. Serve the vegetable stir-fry over the cooked rice. You can garnish with chopped green onions, sesame seeds, or cilantro if desired.
6. Enjoy your delicious Vegetable Stir-Fry with Rice!

Feel free to customize this recipe by adding your favorite vegetables or protein sources such as tofu, tempeh, or cooked chicken or shrimp. It's a great way to use up any leftover vegetables you have on hand and makes for a healthy and satisfying meal.

Bean and Cheese Quesadillas

Ingredients:

- 4 large flour tortillas
- 1 can (15 ounces) of black beans, drained and rinsed
- 1 cup shredded cheese (cheddar, Monterey Jack, or a blend)
- 1/2 cup salsa (optional)
- 1/4 cup chopped fresh cilantro (optional)
- Salt and pepper, to taste
- Cooking spray or vegetable oil, for cooking

Instructions:

1. Heat a large skillet or griddle over medium heat.
2. Place one tortilla on a flat surface. Spread a quarter of the black beans evenly over half of the tortilla, leaving a small border around the edges. Sprinkle a quarter of the shredded cheese over the beans. If using salsa and cilantro, spoon a tablespoon of salsa over the cheese and sprinkle some chopped cilantro on top. Season with salt and pepper, if desired.
3. Fold the empty half of the tortilla over the filling, creating a half-moon shape.
4. Lightly spray the preheated skillet or griddle with cooking spray or brush with a little vegetable oil. Carefully place the filled quesadilla onto the skillet.
5. Cook the quesadilla for 2-3 minutes on each side, or until golden brown and crispy, and the cheese is melted.
6. Remove the cooked quesadilla from the skillet and place it on a cutting board. Allow it to cool for a minute or two before slicing it into wedges.
7. Repeat the process with the remaining tortillas and filling ingredients.
8. Serve the bean and cheese quesadillas warm, with additional salsa, guacamole, sour cream, or your favorite toppings on the side, if desired.

Enjoy your delicious Bean and Cheese Quesadillas! They're perfect for a quick lunch, dinner, or snack, and you can customize them with your favorite ingredients.

Tuna Salad Sandwiches

Ingredients:

- 2 cans (5 ounces each) of tuna, drained
- 1/4 cup mayonnaise
- 2 tablespoons diced red onion
- 2 tablespoons diced celery
- 1 tablespoon chopped fresh parsley
- 1 tablespoon lemon juice
- Salt and pepper, to taste
- 8 slices of bread (white, whole wheat, or your choice)
- Lettuce leaves, tomato slices, and/or avocado slices (optional, for serving)

Instructions:

1. In a mixing bowl, combine the drained tuna, mayonnaise, diced red onion, diced celery, chopped parsley, and lemon juice. Stir until well combined. Season with salt and pepper to taste.
2. Place 4 slices of bread on a clean surface. Divide the tuna salad mixture evenly among the bread slices, spreading it out in an even layer.
3. If desired, top the tuna salad with lettuce leaves, tomato slices, avocado slices, or any other toppings of your choice.
4. Place the remaining 4 slices of bread on top of the tuna salad-topped slices to form sandwiches.
5. If desired, you can cut the sandwiches in half diagonally to serve.
6. Serve the tuna salad sandwiches immediately, or wrap them tightly in plastic wrap or foil for later.

Enjoy your delicious Tuna Salad Sandwiches! They're perfect for a quick lunch, dinner, or picnic, and you can customize them with your favorite toppings and bread.

Lentil Soup

Ingredients:

- 1 cup dried lentils (brown or green), rinsed and drained
- 1 onion, diced
- 2 carrots, diced
- 2 celery stalks, diced
- 2 cloves garlic, minced
- 1 can (14.5 ounces) diced tomatoes
- 4 cups vegetable or chicken broth
- 1 teaspoon ground cumin
- 1 teaspoon ground coriander
- 1/2 teaspoon smoked paprika (optional)
- Salt and pepper, to taste
- 2 tablespoons olive oil
- Fresh parsley or cilantro, chopped (for garnish)
- Lemon wedges (for serving, optional)

Instructions:

1. Heat olive oil in a large pot over medium heat. Add diced onion, carrots, and celery. Cook, stirring occasionally, until vegetables are softened, about 5-7 minutes.
2. Add minced garlic, ground cumin, ground coriander, and smoked paprika (if using). Cook for another 1-2 minutes until fragrant.
3. Add rinsed and drained lentils, diced tomatoes (with their juices), and vegetable or chicken broth to the pot. Stir to combine.
4. Bring the soup to a boil, then reduce the heat to low. Cover and simmer for about 20-25 minutes, or until the lentils are tender.
5. Once the lentils are cooked, season the soup with salt and pepper to taste. Adjust seasoning if needed.
6. If you prefer a smoother consistency, you can use an immersion blender to partially blend the soup, or transfer a portion of the soup to a blender and blend until smooth, then return it to the pot.
7. Serve the lentil soup hot, garnished with chopped fresh parsley or cilantro. You can also squeeze a wedge of lemon over each serving for a burst of freshness, if desired.
8. Enjoy your delicious and comforting Lentil Soup!

This soup pairs well with crusty bread or a side salad for a complete meal. It's also great for meal prep and can be stored in the refrigerator for several days or frozen for longer-term storage.

Veggie Fried Rice

Ingredients:

- 2 cups cooked rice (white or brown), preferably chilled
- 2 tablespoons vegetable oil
- 2 cloves garlic, minced
- 1 small onion, diced
- 2 carrots, diced
- 1 bell pepper (any color), diced
- 1 cup frozen peas, thawed
- 2 eggs, lightly beaten
- 3 tablespoons soy sauce (or tamari for gluten-free)
- 1 tablespoon sesame oil
- Salt and pepper, to taste
- Green onions, chopped, for garnish (optional)
- Sesame seeds, for garnish (optional)

Instructions:

1. Heat 1 tablespoon of vegetable oil in a large skillet or wok over medium-high heat.
2. Add the minced garlic and diced onion to the skillet. Cook, stirring frequently, until the onion is translucent and fragrant, about 2-3 minutes.
3. Add the diced carrots and bell pepper to the skillet. Cook, stirring occasionally, for another 3-4 minutes, or until the vegetables are tender-crisp.
4. Push the vegetables to one side of the skillet, and pour the beaten eggs into the other side. Allow the eggs to cook undisturbed for a minute or two until they start to set. Then, scramble the eggs with a spatula until cooked through.
5. Add the cooked rice and thawed peas to the skillet. Stir everything together until well combined.
6. Drizzle the soy sauce and sesame oil over the rice mixture. Stir to evenly distribute the sauce and coat the rice.
7. Continue cooking, stirring frequently, for another 3-4 minutes, or until the rice is heated through and starts to turn slightly crispy.
8. Taste the fried rice and season with salt and pepper to taste, if needed.
9. Remove the skillet from the heat. Garnish the fried rice with chopped green onions and sesame seeds, if desired.
10. Serve the veggie fried rice hot as a delicious and satisfying meal or side dish.

Enjoy your flavorful Veggie Fried Rice! It's a versatile dish that you can customize with your favorite vegetables and protein sources, such as tofu or cooked chicken or shrimp.

Baked Potato with Beans and Cheese

Ingredients:

- 4 large baking potatoes
- 1 can (15 ounces) of your favorite beans (such as black beans, kidney beans, or pinto beans), drained and rinsed
- 1 cup shredded cheese (cheddar, Monterey Jack, or your favorite cheese blend)
- 1/4 cup sour cream (optional)
- 2 green onions, chopped (optional)
- Salt and pepper, to taste
- Olive oil, for rubbing the potatoes

Instructions:

1. Preheat your oven to 400°F (200°C). Scrub the potatoes clean under running water and pat them dry with a kitchen towel.
2. Pierce each potato several times with a fork or knife to allow steam to escape during baking. Rub the potatoes with a little olive oil and sprinkle with salt.
3. Place the potatoes directly on the oven rack or on a baking sheet lined with aluminum foil. Bake for 45-60 minutes, or until the potatoes are tender when pierced with a fork.
4. While the potatoes are baking, prepare the bean and cheese topping. In a small saucepan, heat the drained and rinsed beans over medium heat until heated through. Season with salt and pepper to taste.
5. Once the potatoes are cooked, remove them from the oven and let them cool slightly for a few minutes.
6. To serve, carefully slice each baked potato lengthwise down the center, without cutting all the way through. Use your fingers to gently squeeze the ends of the potato towards the middle to open up a space for the toppings.
7. Spoon the heated beans over the opened potatoes, dividing them evenly among the potatoes.
8. Sprinkle shredded cheese over the beans on each potato, allowing the cheese to melt slightly from the heat of the beans.
9. If desired, top each potato with a dollop of sour cream and a sprinkle of chopped green onions.
10. Serve the baked potatoes with beans and cheese hot as a satisfying and delicious meal.

Enjoy your flavorful Baked Potatoes with Beans and Cheese! They're perfect for a comforting lunch or dinner. You can also customize them with additional toppings such as salsa, guacamole, or diced tomatoes.

Pasta Primavera

Ingredients:

- 12 ounces pasta (linguine, fettuccine, or your favorite pasta shape)
- 2 tablespoons olive oil
- 2 cloves garlic, minced
- 1 small onion, thinly sliced
- 2 carrots, julienned or thinly sliced
- 1 bell pepper (any color), thinly sliced
- 1 small zucchini, halved lengthwise and thinly sliced
- 1 small yellow squash, halved lengthwise and thinly sliced
- 1 cup cherry tomatoes, halved
- 1 cup broccoli florets
- 1 cup asparagus spears, trimmed and cut into 2-inch pieces
- 1/2 cup vegetable broth or pasta cooking water
- 1/4 cup grated Parmesan cheese
- Salt and pepper, to taste
- Fresh basil or parsley, chopped, for garnish (optional)

Instructions:

1. Cook the pasta according to the package instructions in a large pot of salted boiling water until al dente. Reserve about 1/2 cup of pasta cooking water before draining.
2. While the pasta is cooking, heat the olive oil in a large skillet over medium heat. Add the minced garlic and sliced onion to the skillet. Cook, stirring occasionally, until the onion is translucent and fragrant, about 2-3 minutes.
3. Add the julienned carrots, sliced bell pepper, sliced zucchini, sliced yellow squash, cherry tomatoes, broccoli florets, and asparagus pieces to the skillet. Cook, stirring frequently, for 5-7 minutes, or until the vegetables are tender-crisp.
4. Once the vegetables are cooked, add the cooked pasta to the skillet along with the vegetable broth or pasta cooking water. Toss everything together until well combined.
5. Stir in the grated Parmesan cheese, and season with salt and pepper to taste. If the pasta seems dry, you can add a little more vegetable broth or pasta cooking water.
6. Cook for an additional 1-2 minutes, allowing the flavors to meld together.

7. Remove the skillet from the heat. Garnish the pasta primavera with chopped fresh basil or parsley, if desired.
8. Serve the pasta primavera hot, with additional grated Parmesan cheese on top if desired.

Enjoy your vibrant and delicious Pasta Primavera! It's a perfect dish to showcase the fresh flavors of spring and makes for a satisfying meal.

Black Bean Tacos

Ingredients:

For the Black Beans:

- 2 cans (15 ounces each) black beans, drained and rinsed
- 1 tablespoon olive oil
- 1 small onion, finely chopped
- 2 cloves garlic, minced
- 1 teaspoon ground cumin
- 1 teaspoon chili powder
- 1/2 teaspoon paprika
- Salt and pepper, to taste
- 1/4 cup chopped fresh cilantro (optional)
- Juice of 1 lime (optional)

For Serving:

- 8-10 small corn or flour tortillas
- Toppings of your choice, such as:
    - Shredded lettuce or cabbage
    - Diced tomatoes
    - Diced avocado or guacamole
    - Sliced jalapeños
    - Chopped fresh cilantro
    - Salsa or pico de gallo
    - Sour cream or Greek yogurt
    - Crumbled feta or shredded cheese

Instructions:

1. Heat olive oil in a large skillet over medium heat. Add chopped onion and minced garlic, and sauté until softened and fragrant, about 3-4 minutes.
2. Add drained and rinsed black beans to the skillet, along with ground cumin, chili powder, paprika, salt, and pepper. Stir well to combine.

3. Cook the black bean mixture for 5-7 minutes, stirring occasionally, until heated through and the flavors are well blended. If the mixture seems too dry, you can add a splash of water or vegetable broth.
4. If using, add chopped fresh cilantro and lime juice to the black bean mixture, and stir to combine. Remove the skillet from heat.
5. Warm the tortillas according to package instructions or heat them briefly in a dry skillet until soft and pliable.
6. Assemble the tacos by spooning the black bean mixture onto each tortilla. Top with your desired toppings, such as shredded lettuce, diced tomatoes, diced avocado, sliced jalapeños, chopped cilantro, salsa, sour cream, or shredded cheese.
7. Serve the black bean tacos immediately, with lime wedges on the side for squeezing over the tacos, if desired.

Enjoy your delicious and customizable Black Bean Tacos! They're perfect for a quick and flavorful weeknight dinner or for entertaining guests.

Tomato and Basil Bruschetta

Ingredients:

- 4-6 ripe tomatoes, diced
- 1/4 cup fresh basil leaves, chopped
- 2 cloves garlic, minced
- 2 tablespoons extra virgin olive oil
- 1 tablespoon balsamic vinegar (optional)
- Salt and pepper, to taste
- 1 baguette or Italian bread, sliced into 1/2-inch thick slices
- Olive oil, for brushing
- 1 clove garlic, peeled (optional, for rubbing on the bread)

Instructions:

1. Preheat the oven to 400°F (200°C). Arrange the sliced baguette or Italian bread on a baking sheet in a single layer.
2. Brush the bread slices lightly with olive oil on both sides. Optionally, you can rub each slice of bread with a peeled clove of garlic for extra flavor.
3. Bake the bread slices in the preheated oven for 5-7 minutes, or until they are golden brown and crisp. Remove from the oven and set aside to cool slightly.
4. In a mixing bowl, combine the diced tomatoes, chopped basil, minced garlic, extra virgin olive oil, and balsamic vinegar (if using). Season with salt and pepper to taste. Stir gently to combine all the ingredients.
5. Allow the tomato and basil mixture to marinate for at least 10-15 minutes to allow the flavors to meld together.
6. Once the bread slices have cooled slightly, spoon the tomato and basil mixture generously onto each slice.
7. Serve the Tomato and Basil Bruschetta immediately as a delicious appetizer or snack.

Enjoy your fresh and flavorful Tomato and Basil Bruschetta! It's perfect for entertaining guests or as a light and tasty starter before a meal.

Chickpea Curry with Rice

Ingredients:

For the Chickpea Curry:

- 2 tablespoons vegetable oil
- 1 onion, finely chopped
- 3 cloves garlic, minced
- 1 tablespoon fresh ginger, grated
- 1 tablespoon curry powder
- 1 teaspoon ground cumin
- 1 teaspoon ground coriander
- 1/2 teaspoon turmeric powder
- 1/4 teaspoon cayenne pepper (adjust to taste)
- 1 can (15 ounces) chickpeas, drained and rinsed
- 1 can (14.5 ounces) diced tomatoes
- 1 can (13.5 ounces) coconut milk
- Salt, to taste
- Fresh cilantro, chopped, for garnish (optional)

For Serving:

- Cooked rice (white or brown)
- Naan bread or roti (optional)

Instructions:

1. Heat vegetable oil in a large skillet or pot over medium heat. Add finely chopped onion and cook until softened and translucent, about 5-7 minutes.
2. Add minced garlic and grated ginger to the skillet. Cook for another 1-2 minutes until fragrant.
3. Stir in curry powder, ground cumin, ground coriander, turmeric powder, and cayenne pepper. Cook, stirring constantly, for about 1 minute to toast the spices.
4. Add drained and rinsed chickpeas to the skillet, along with diced tomatoes (with their juices) and coconut milk. Stir to combine all the ingredients.
5. Bring the mixture to a simmer, then reduce the heat to low. Cover and let the curry simmer gently for about 15-20 minutes to allow the flavors to meld together and the sauce to thicken slightly.
6. Taste the chickpea curry and season with salt to taste.

7. Serve the chickpea curry hot over cooked rice. Garnish with chopped fresh cilantro, if desired.
8. Serve with naan bread or roti on the side, if desired, for scooping up the curry.

Enjoy your delicious Chickpea Curry with Rice! It's a comforting and flavorful meal that's perfect for a weeknight dinner or for entertaining guests.

Greek Salad with Pita Bread

Ingredients:

For the Greek Salad:

- 4 large tomatoes, diced
- 1 English cucumber, diced
- 1 red onion, thinly sliced
- 1 green bell pepper, diced
- 1/2 cup Kalamata olives, pitted
- 1/2 cup crumbled feta cheese
- 1/4 cup fresh parsley, chopped
- 2 tablespoons extra virgin olive oil
- 1 tablespoon red wine vinegar
- Salt and pepper, to taste

For Serving:

- Pita bread, warmed
- Additional olive oil and vinegar, for drizzling (optional)

Instructions:

1. In a large mixing bowl, combine diced tomatoes, diced cucumber, thinly sliced red onion, diced green bell pepper, pitted Kalamata olives, crumbled feta cheese, and chopped fresh parsley.
2. Drizzle extra virgin olive oil and red wine vinegar over the salad ingredients. Toss gently to coat everything evenly.
3. Season the Greek salad with salt and pepper to taste. Adjust seasoning if needed.
4. Let the salad marinate for about 10-15 minutes at room temperature to allow the flavors to meld together.
5. While the salad is marinating, warm the pita bread in a toaster oven or on a grill until heated through and slightly crispy.
6. Once the pita bread is warmed, cut it into wedges.
7. To serve, arrange the Greek salad on a serving platter or individual plates. Place the warmed pita bread wedges alongside the salad.
8. If desired, drizzle a little extra olive oil and vinegar over the salad and pita bread before serving.

9. Serve the Greek Salad with Pita Bread immediately as a refreshing and satisfying meal or side dish.

Enjoy your delicious Greek Salad with Pita Bread! It's packed with fresh flavors and makes for a perfect light and healthy meal.

Egg Fried Rice

Ingredients:

- 3 cups cooked rice (white or brown), preferably chilled
- 3 tablespoons vegetable oil
- 2-3 large eggs, lightly beaten
- 1 cup mixed vegetables (such as peas, carrots, corn, and bell peppers), diced
- 2 cloves garlic, minced
- 2 green onions, thinly sliced
- 2 tablespoons soy sauce (or more to taste)
- 1 tablespoon oyster sauce (optional)
- Salt and pepper, to taste
- Sesame oil, for drizzling (optional)
- Toasted sesame seeds, for garnish (optional)
- Chopped fresh cilantro or parsley, for garnish (optional)

Instructions:

1. Heat 1 tablespoon of vegetable oil in a large skillet or wok over medium heat. Add the beaten eggs and cook, stirring gently, until scrambled and cooked through. Transfer the scrambled eggs to a plate and set aside.
2. Wipe the skillet or wok clean and heat the remaining 2 tablespoons of vegetable oil over medium-high heat. Add the minced garlic and diced mixed vegetables to the skillet. Stir-fry for 3-4 minutes, or until the vegetables are tender-crisp.
3. Add the chilled cooked rice to the skillet. Break up any clumps of rice with a spatula and stir-fry for 2-3 minutes to heat through.
4. Push the rice to one side of the skillet and pour the beaten eggs into the empty space. Allow the eggs to cook undisturbed for a minute or two until they start to set. Then, scramble the eggs with a spatula until cooked through.
5. Once the eggs are cooked, stir them into the rice mixture in the skillet.
6. Add soy sauce and oyster sauce (if using) to the skillet, stirring well to coat the rice evenly. Season with salt and pepper to taste.
7. Continue to stir-fry the rice mixture for another 2-3 minutes, or until everything is heated through and well combined.
8. Remove the skillet from the heat. Drizzle with a little sesame oil for extra flavor, if desired.
9. Garnish the Egg Fried Rice with sliced green onions, toasted sesame seeds, and chopped fresh cilantro or parsley, if desired.
10. Serve the Egg Fried Rice hot as a delicious and satisfying meal or side dish.

Enjoy your flavorful and comforting Egg Fried Rice! It's a versatile dish that you can customize with your favorite vegetables and protein sources.

Vegetable Frittata

Ingredients:

- 8 large eggs
- 1/4 cup milk or heavy cream
- Salt and pepper, to taste
- 2 tablespoons olive oil
- 1 small onion, diced
- 2 cloves garlic, minced
- 2 cups mixed vegetables (such as bell peppers, spinach, mushrooms, tomatoes, zucchini, etc.), diced or sliced
- 1/2 cup shredded cheese (such as cheddar, mozzarella, or feta)
- Fresh herbs (such as parsley, basil, or chives), chopped, for garnish (optional)

Instructions:

1. Preheat your oven to 350°F (175°C).
2. In a large mixing bowl, whisk together the eggs and milk or heavy cream until well combined. Season with salt and pepper to taste. Set aside.
3. Heat olive oil in a 10-inch oven-safe skillet over medium heat. Add diced onion and cook until softened and translucent, about 3-4 minutes.
4. Add minced garlic to the skillet and cook for another 1-2 minutes until fragrant.
5. Add the diced or sliced mixed vegetables to the skillet. Cook, stirring occasionally, until the vegetables are tender-crisp, about 5-7 minutes.
6. Spread the cooked vegetables evenly in the skillet. Sprinkle shredded cheese over the vegetables.
7. Pour the whisked egg mixture evenly over the vegetables and cheese in the skillet.
8. Cook the frittata on the stovetop for 3-4 minutes, or until the edges start to set.
9. Transfer the skillet to the preheated oven and bake the frittata for 12-15 minutes, or until the eggs are set in the center and the top is lightly golden brown.
10. Once the frittata is cooked, remove it from the oven and let it cool slightly in the skillet for a few minutes.
11. Carefully slide a spatula around the edges of the skillet to loosen the frittata. Slide the frittata onto a cutting board.

12. Slice the frittata into wedges or squares. Garnish with chopped fresh herbs, if desired.
13. Serve the Vegetable Frittata warm or at room temperature as a delicious and satisfying meal.

Enjoy your flavorful and nutritious Vegetable Frittata! It's a great way to use up leftover vegetables and can be customized with your favorite ingredients.

Black Bean Soup

Ingredients:

- 2 cans (15 ounces each) black beans, drained and rinsed
- 2 tablespoons olive oil
- 1 onion, chopped
- 2 cloves garlic, minced
- 1 bell pepper (any color), chopped
- 1 jalapeño pepper, seeded and diced (optional, for heat)
- 2 teaspoons ground cumin
- 1 teaspoon chili powder
- 1/2 teaspoon smoked paprika
- 4 cups vegetable or chicken broth
- 1 can (14.5 ounces) diced tomatoes
- Salt and pepper, to taste
- Juice of 1 lime
- Fresh cilantro, chopped, for garnish (optional)
- Sour cream or Greek yogurt, for garnish (optional)
- Avocado slices, for garnish (optional)
- Tortilla chips or crusty bread, for serving

Instructions:

1. In a large pot or Dutch oven, heat olive oil over medium heat. Add chopped onion and cook until softened, about 5 minutes.
2. Add minced garlic, chopped bell pepper, and diced jalapeño pepper (if using). Cook for another 2-3 minutes, until fragrant.
3. Stir in ground cumin, chili powder, and smoked paprika. Cook for 1 minute, stirring constantly, to toast the spices.
4. Add drained and rinsed black beans to the pot, along with vegetable or chicken broth and diced tomatoes (with their juices). Stir to combine.
5. Bring the soup to a simmer, then reduce the heat to low. Cover and let the soup simmer gently for about 20-25 minutes to allow the flavors to meld together.
6. After simmering, use an immersion blender to partially blend the soup until it reaches your desired consistency. Alternatively, you can transfer a portion of the soup to a blender and blend until smooth, then return it to the pot.
7. Season the soup with salt and pepper to taste. Stir in the juice of 1 lime.
8. Ladle the Black Bean Soup into bowls. Garnish with chopped fresh cilantro, a dollop of sour cream or Greek yogurt, and avocado slices, if desired.
9. Serve the soup hot, with tortilla chips or crusty bread on the side for dipping.

Enjoy your delicious and comforting Black Bean Soup! It's a nutritious and satisfying meal that's perfect for any occasion.

Margherita Pizza

Ingredients:

- 1 pizza dough (store-bought or homemade)
- 1/2 cup pizza sauce or marinara sauce
- 8 ounces fresh mozzarella cheese, sliced
- 2-3 large tomatoes, thinly sliced
- Fresh basil leaves, torn or chopped
- Extra-virgin olive oil
- Salt and pepper, to taste

Instructions:

1. Preheat your oven to the highest temperature setting (usually around 500°F or as high as your oven can go) and place a pizza stone or baking sheet in the oven to preheat.
2. Roll out the pizza dough on a lightly floured surface to your desired thickness. Transfer the dough to a piece of parchment paper.
3. Spread the pizza sauce evenly over the dough, leaving a small border around the edges.
4. Arrange the sliced fresh mozzarella cheese evenly over the sauce.
5. Place the thinly sliced tomatoes on top of the cheese, overlapping slightly.
6. Season the tomatoes with salt and pepper to taste.
7. Drizzle a little extra-virgin olive oil over the pizza.
8. Carefully transfer the pizza (on the parchment paper) to the preheated pizza stone or baking sheet in the oven.
9. Bake the pizza for 10-12 minutes, or until the crust is golden brown and the cheese is bubbly and melted.
10. Remove the pizza from the oven and sprinkle torn or chopped fresh basil leaves over the top.
11. Let the pizza cool for a minute or two before slicing.
12. Serve the Margherita Pizza hot and enjoy!

This classic Margherita Pizza celebrates the flavors of fresh tomatoes, creamy mozzarella cheese, and aromatic basil. It's simple yet incredibly delicious!

Caprese Salad

Ingredients:

- 2 large ripe tomatoes, sliced
- 8 ounces fresh mozzarella cheese, sliced
- Fresh basil leaves
- Extra-virgin olive oil, for drizzling
- Balsamic glaze or balsamic vinegar reduction (optional)
- Salt and pepper, to taste

Instructions:

1. Arrange the tomato slices and mozzarella cheese slices alternately on a serving platter, overlapping slightly.
2. Tuck fresh basil leaves in between the tomato and mozzarella slices.
3. Drizzle extra-virgin olive oil over the tomato and mozzarella slices.
4. If using, drizzle balsamic glaze or balsamic vinegar reduction over the salad for added sweetness and flavor (optional).
5. Season the salad with salt and pepper to taste.
6. Serve the Caprese Salad immediately as a refreshing and flavorful appetizer or side dish.

Enjoy your delicious and classic Caprese Salad! It's perfect for showcasing the flavors of ripe tomatoes, creamy mozzarella, and aromatic basil.

Spinach and Feta Quesadillas

Ingredients:

- 4 large flour tortillas
- 2 cups fresh spinach leaves, chopped
- 1/2 cup crumbled feta cheese
- 1/4 cup shredded mozzarella cheese (optional)
- 1/4 cup chopped sun-dried tomatoes (optional)
- 1/4 cup chopped red onion (optional)
- 1 tablespoon olive oil or butter, for cooking

Instructions:

1. In a mixing bowl, combine chopped spinach, crumbled feta cheese, shredded mozzarella cheese (if using), chopped sun-dried tomatoes (if using), and chopped red onion (if using). Stir to evenly distribute the ingredients.
2. Heat a large skillet or griddle over medium heat. Brush one side of each tortilla lightly with olive oil or spread a thin layer of butter.
3. Place one tortilla, oiled side down, in the preheated skillet. Spread a quarter of the spinach and feta mixture evenly over half of the tortilla, leaving a small border around the edges.
4. Fold the empty half of the tortilla over the filling, creating a half-moon shape.
5. Cook the quesadilla for 2-3 minutes on each side, or until golden brown and crispy, and the cheese is melted.
6. Remove the cooked quesadilla from the skillet and place it on a cutting board. Allow it to cool for a minute or two before slicing it into wedges.
7. Repeat the process with the remaining tortillas and filling ingredients.
8. Serve the Spinach and Feta Quesadillas warm, with additional toppings such as salsa, guacamole, or sour cream on the side, if desired.

Enjoy your delicious Spinach and Feta Quesadillas! They're perfect for a quick and satisfying lunch or dinner, and you can customize them with your favorite ingredients.

Tomato Soup with Grilled Cheese Sandwiches

Ingredients:

- 2 tablespoons olive oil
- 1 onion, chopped
- 2 cloves garlic, minced
- 1 can (28 ounces) crushed tomatoes
- 2 cups vegetable or chicken broth
- 1 teaspoon dried basil
- 1 teaspoon dried oregano
- Salt and pepper, to taste
- 1/2 cup heavy cream or half-and-half (optional, for creamier soup)
- Fresh basil leaves, chopped, for garnish (optional)

Instructions:

1. In a large pot, heat olive oil over medium heat. Add chopped onion and cook until softened, about 5 minutes.
2. Add minced garlic to the pot and cook for another 1-2 minutes until fragrant.
3. Stir in crushed tomatoes, vegetable or chicken broth, dried basil, and dried oregano. Season with salt and pepper to taste.
4. Bring the soup to a simmer, then reduce the heat to low. Cover and let the soup simmer gently for about 15-20 minutes to allow the flavors to meld together.
5. If using, stir in heavy cream or half-and-half to make the soup creamier.
6. Use an immersion blender to puree the soup until smooth. Alternatively, you can transfer the soup in batches to a blender and blend until smooth, then return it to the pot.
7. Taste the soup and adjust seasoning if needed.
8. Serve the tomato soup hot, garnished with chopped fresh basil leaves if desired.

Grilled Cheese Sandwiches

Ingredients:

- 8 slices of bread (white, whole wheat, or your choice)
- 8 slices of cheese (cheddar, American, Swiss, or your favorite cheese)
- Butter or margarine, softened

Instructions:

1. Heat a large skillet or griddle over medium heat.
2. Spread softened butter or margarine evenly over one side of each slice of bread.
3. Place four slices of bread, buttered side down, on the skillet or griddle. Top each slice with a slice of cheese.
4. Place the remaining four slices of bread, buttered side up, on top of the cheese.
5. Cook the sandwiches for 3-4 minutes on each side, or until the bread is golden brown and crispy, and the cheese is melted.
6. Once the sandwiches are cooked, remove them from the skillet and let them cool for a minute or two before slicing them in half.
7. Serve the grilled cheese sandwiches hot, alongside the tomato soup.

Enjoy your comforting Tomato Soup with Grilled Cheese Sandwiches! It's a classic combination that's sure to warm you up on a chilly day.

Mushroom Risotto

Ingredients:

- 6 cups vegetable or chicken broth
- 2 tablespoons olive oil
- 1 onion, finely chopped
- 2 cloves garlic, minced
- 1 pound (about 450g) mushrooms (such as cremini, shiitake, or button mushrooms), sliced
- 2 cups Arborio rice
- 1/2 cup dry white wine (optional)
- 1/2 cup grated Parmesan cheese
- 2 tablespoons unsalted butter
- Salt and pepper, to taste
- Fresh parsley, chopped, for garnish (optional)

Instructions:

1. In a medium saucepan, heat the vegetable or chicken broth over medium heat. Once hot, reduce the heat to low to keep it warm.
2. In a large skillet or sauté pan, heat the olive oil over medium heat. Add the chopped onion and cook until softened, about 5 minutes.
3. Add the minced garlic to the skillet and cook for another minute until fragrant.
4. Add the sliced mushrooms to the skillet and cook, stirring occasionally, until they release their moisture and begin to brown, about 8-10 minutes.
5. Stir in the Arborio rice and cook for 1-2 minutes, stirring constantly, until the rice is lightly toasted.
6. If using, pour in the dry white wine and cook, stirring, until the wine has evaporated.
7. Begin adding the warm broth to the skillet, one ladleful at a time, stirring frequently and allowing each addition of broth to be absorbed before adding more. Continue this process until the rice is creamy and tender, but still slightly al dente, about 20-25 minutes.
8. Once the rice is cooked to your liking, remove the skillet from the heat. Stir in the grated Parmesan cheese and unsalted butter until melted and creamy. Season with salt and pepper to taste.
9. Serve the Mushroom Risotto hot, garnished with chopped fresh parsley if desired.

Enjoy your creamy and flavorful Mushroom Risotto! It's perfect as a main dish or as a side to complement your favorite protein.

Potato and Pea Samosas

Ingredients:

For the filling:

- 2 large potatoes, boiled, peeled, and diced
- 1 cup green peas (fresh or frozen)
- 1 tablespoon vegetable oil
- 1 teaspoon cumin seeds
- 1 teaspoon coriander powder
- 1/2 teaspoon turmeric powder
- 1/2 teaspoon garam masala
- 1/2 teaspoon chili powder (adjust to taste)
- Salt, to taste
- 2 tablespoons chopped fresh coriander (cilantro) leaves
- 1 tablespoon lemon juice

For the pastry:

- 2 cups all-purpose flour
- 1/2 teaspoon salt
- 4 tablespoons vegetable oil or melted ghee
- Water, as needed

Instructions:

1. To make the filling, heat the vegetable oil in a large skillet over medium heat. Add the cumin seeds and cook until they start to sizzle.
2. Add the diced potatoes to the skillet and sauté for a few minutes until lightly golden.
3. Stir in the green peas, coriander powder, turmeric powder, garam masala, chili powder, and salt. Cook for another 2-3 minutes until the peas are tender.
4. Remove the skillet from the heat and stir in the chopped fresh coriander (cilantro) leaves and lemon juice. Set the filling aside to cool.
5. To make the pastry, in a large mixing bowl, combine the all-purpose flour and salt. Gradually add the vegetable oil or melted ghee and mix until the flour resembles breadcrumbs.

6. Gradually add water, a little at a time, and knead until a smooth and pliable dough forms. Cover the dough with a damp cloth and let it rest for 30 minutes.
7. Divide the dough into small balls, about the size of golf balls.
8. Roll out each ball of dough into a thin circle, about 6 inches in diameter.
9. Cut each circle in half to form two semi-circles.
10. Take one semi-circle and fold it into a cone shape, overlapping the edges slightly. Seal the edges by pressing them together.
11. Fill the cone with a spoonful of the potato and pea filling.
12. Brush the edges of the cone with a little water and press them together to seal the samosa.
13. Repeat the process with the remaining dough and filling.
14. Heat vegetable oil in a deep frying pan or pot over medium-high heat. Once the oil is hot, fry the samosas in batches until they are golden brown and crispy, about 3-4 minutes per side.
15. Remove the samosas from the oil and drain them on paper towels.
16. Serve the Potato and Pea Samosas hot with your favorite chutney or dipping sauce.

Enjoy your delicious homemade Potato and Pea Samosas! They're perfect as a snack or appetizer for any occasion.

Vegetarian Chili

Ingredients:

- 2 tablespoons olive oil
- 1 onion, diced
- 3 cloves garlic, minced
- 1 bell pepper (any color), diced
- 2 carrots, diced
- 2 stalks celery, diced
- 1 zucchini, diced
- 1 yellow squash, diced
- 1 can (15 ounces) black beans, drained and rinsed
- 1 can (15 ounces) kidney beans, drained and rinsed
- 1 can (15 ounces) pinto beans, drained and rinsed
- 1 can (28 ounces) crushed tomatoes
- 2 cups vegetable broth
- 2 tablespoons tomato paste
- 2 teaspoons chili powder
- 1 teaspoon ground cumin
- 1 teaspoon paprika
- 1/2 teaspoon dried oregano
- Salt and pepper, to taste
- Optional toppings: shredded cheese, chopped fresh cilantro, sliced green onions, sour cream, avocado

Instructions:

1. In a large pot or Dutch oven, heat the olive oil over medium heat. Add the diced onion and cook until softened, about 5 minutes.
2. Add the minced garlic to the pot and cook for another minute until fragrant.
3. Add the diced bell pepper, carrots, celery, zucchini, and yellow squash to the pot. Cook, stirring occasionally, for about 5-7 minutes until the vegetables start to soften.
4. Stir in the drained and rinsed black beans, kidney beans, and pinto beans.
5. Add the crushed tomatoes, vegetable broth, tomato paste, chili powder, ground cumin, paprika, dried oregano, salt, and pepper to the pot. Stir well to combine all the ingredients.
6. Bring the chili to a simmer, then reduce the heat to low. Cover and let the chili simmer gently for about 30-40 minutes, stirring occasionally, until the vegetables are tender and the flavors have melded together.
7. Taste the chili and adjust seasoning if needed.

8. Serve the vegetarian chili hot, garnished with your favorite toppings such as shredded cheese, chopped fresh cilantro, sliced green onions, sour cream, or avocado.

Enjoy your hearty and flavorful Vegetarian Chili! It's perfect for a cozy meal on a chilly day, and you can customize it with your favorite beans and vegetables.

Falafel with Hummus and Pita

Ingredients:

For the falafel:

- 1 cup dried chickpeas, soaked overnight
- 1/2 onion, roughly chopped
- 3 cloves garlic, minced
- 1/4 cup fresh parsley, chopped
- 1/4 cup fresh cilantro, chopped
- 1 teaspoon ground cumin
- 1 teaspoon ground coriander
- 1/2 teaspoon baking powder
- Salt and pepper, to taste
- Vegetable oil, for frying

For the hummus:

- 1 can (15 ounces) chickpeas, drained and rinsed
- 1/4 cup tahini
- 2 tablespoons lemon juice
- 2 cloves garlic, minced
- 2 tablespoons olive oil
- Salt, to taste
- Water, as needed

For serving:

- Pita bread
- Sliced tomatoes
- Sliced cucumbers
- Chopped lettuce
- Sliced red onion
- Pickles
- Hot sauce or tahini sauce (optional)

Instructions:

1. To make the falafel, drain the soaked chickpeas and pat them dry with paper towels. In a food processor, combine the chickpeas, onion, garlic, parsley, cilantro, ground cumin, ground coriander, baking powder, salt, and pepper. Pulse until the mixture is coarsely ground and holds together when squeezed.
2. Transfer the falafel mixture to a bowl, cover, and refrigerate for at least 1 hour to firm up.
3. Meanwhile, make the hummus. In a food processor, combine the drained and rinsed chickpeas, tahini, lemon juice, minced garlic, olive oil, and salt. Process until smooth, adding water as needed to achieve your desired consistency. Taste and adjust seasoning if needed.
4. Heat vegetable oil in a deep fryer or large skillet to 350°F (175°C).
5. Shape the chilled falafel mixture into small balls or patties, about 1 1/2 inches in diameter.
6. Carefully lower the falafel balls or patties into the hot oil in batches, and fry until golden brown and crispy, about 3-4 minutes per batch. Remove with a slotted spoon and drain on paper towels.
7. Warm the pita bread in a toaster oven or on a skillet until soft and pliable.
8. To serve, spread a generous amount of hummus on each pita bread round. Top with falafel, sliced tomatoes, sliced cucumbers, chopped lettuce, sliced red onion, and pickles. Drizzle with hot sauce or tahini sauce, if desired.
9. Roll up the pita bread to enclose the filling, or serve open-faced.
10. Serve the falafel with hummus and pita immediately, while still warm.

Enjoy your delicious homemade Falafel with Hummus and Pita! It's a perfect combination of flavors and textures that's sure to satisfy your cravings for Middle Eastern cuisine.

Cheese and Spinach Stuffed Shells

Ingredients:

- 20 jumbo pasta shells
- 2 cups ricotta cheese
- 1 cup shredded mozzarella cheese
- 1 cup grated Parmesan cheese, divided
- 1 egg, lightly beaten
- 2 cups fresh spinach, chopped
- 2 cloves garlic, minced
- 1 tablespoon olive oil
- 1 teaspoon dried basil
- 1 teaspoon dried oregano
- Salt and pepper, to taste
- 2 cups marinara sauce
- Fresh basil leaves, chopped, for garnish (optional)

Instructions:

1. Preheat your oven to 350°F (175°C). Cook the jumbo pasta shells according to the package instructions until al dente. Drain and set aside to cool.
2. In a large mixing bowl, combine the ricotta cheese, shredded mozzarella cheese, 1/2 cup of grated Parmesan cheese, and beaten egg. Mix well until smooth and well combined.
3. In a skillet, heat olive oil over medium heat. Add minced garlic and cook for about 1 minute until fragrant. Add chopped spinach and cook until wilted, about 2-3 minutes. Season with dried basil, dried oregano, salt, and pepper.
4. Add the cooked spinach mixture to the cheese mixture and stir until evenly combined.
5. Spread a thin layer of marinara sauce on the bottom of a 9x13-inch baking dish.
6. Stuff each cooked pasta shell with the cheese and spinach mixture, filling them generously. Place the stuffed shells in the baking dish in a single layer.
7. Pour the remaining marinara sauce over the stuffed shells, covering them evenly.
8. Sprinkle the remaining 1/2 cup of grated Parmesan cheese over the top.
9. Cover the baking dish with aluminum foil and bake in the preheated oven for 25-30 minutes, or until the shells are heated through and the cheese is melted and bubbly.
10. Remove the foil and bake for an additional 5-10 minutes, or until the cheese is golden brown.
11. Remove from the oven and let it cool for a few minutes before serving.
12. Garnish with chopped fresh basil leaves, if desired, before serving.

Enjoy your cheesy and flavorful Cheese and Spinach Stuffed Shells! It's a crowd-pleasing dish that's perfect for family dinners or entertaining guests.

Veggie Omelette with Toast

Ingredients:

For the omelette:

- 3 eggs
- 1/4 cup milk (optional)
- Salt and pepper, to taste
- 1 tablespoon butter or oil
- 1/4 cup chopped vegetables (such as bell peppers, onions, tomatoes, spinach, mushrooms, etc.)
- 1/4 cup shredded cheese (optional)

For the toast:

- 2 slices of bread (your choice)
- Butter or margarine, for spreading (optional)

Instructions:

1. In a small bowl, beat the eggs with milk (if using), salt, and pepper until well combined.
2. Heat butter or oil in a non-stick skillet over medium heat.
3. Add the chopped vegetables to the skillet and cook until they are tender, about 3-5 minutes.
4. Pour the beaten eggs over the cooked vegetables in the skillet.
5. Allow the eggs to cook undisturbed for a minute or two until the edges start to set.
6. Using a spatula, gently lift the edges of the omelette and tilt the skillet to let the uncooked eggs flow to the edges.
7. Once the omelette is mostly set but still slightly runny on top, sprinkle shredded cheese (if using) over one half of the omelette.
8. Carefully fold the other half of the omelette over the cheese to form a half-moon shape.
9. Cook for another minute or two until the cheese melts and the omelette is cooked through.
10. Remove the omelette from the skillet and transfer it to a plate.

11. Meanwhile, toast the bread slices until golden brown. Spread butter or margarine on the toast, if desired.
12. Serve the veggie omelette hot with toasted bread on the side.

Enjoy your delicious veggie omelette with toast! You can customize the omelette with your favorite vegetables and cheese for added flavor.

Broccoli Cheddar Soup

Ingredients:

- 4 cups broccoli florets (about 2 small heads)
- 3 tablespoons unsalted butter
- 1 onion, chopped
- 2 cloves garlic, minced
- 1/4 cup all-purpose flour
- 4 cups vegetable or chicken broth
- 2 cups milk
- 2 cups shredded cheddar cheese
- Salt and pepper, to taste
- Pinch of nutmeg (optional)

Instructions:

1. In a large pot, melt the butter over medium heat. Add the chopped onion and cook until softened, about 5 minutes.
2. Add the minced garlic to the pot and cook for another minute until fragrant.
3. Sprinkle the flour over the onions and garlic in the pot. Cook, stirring constantly, for about 2 minutes to cook out the raw flour taste.
4. Gradually whisk in the vegetable or chicken broth until smooth and well combined.
5. Add the milk to the pot and stir until combined. Bring the mixture to a simmer.
6. Add the broccoli florets to the pot and simmer for about 10-15 minutes, or until the broccoli is tender.
7. Use an immersion blender to blend the soup until smooth, or transfer the soup in batches to a blender and blend until smooth. Alternatively, you can leave the soup chunky if desired.
8. Return the soup to the pot if necessary and bring it back to a simmer over medium heat.
9. Stir in the shredded cheddar cheese until melted and smooth. Season with salt, pepper, and a pinch of nutmeg if desired.
10. Taste the soup and adjust seasoning if needed.
11. Serve the broccoli cheddar soup hot, garnished with extra shredded cheese if desired.

Enjoy your creamy and delicious homemade Broccoli Cheddar Soup! It pairs perfectly with crusty bread or crackers for dipping.

Rice and Bean Burritos

Ingredients:

- 1 cup cooked rice (white or brown)
- 1 can (15 ounces) black beans, drained and rinsed
- 1/2 onion, diced
- 2 cloves garlic, minced
- 1 teaspoon ground cumin
- 1/2 teaspoon chili powder
- Salt and pepper, to taste
- 1 cup shredded cheese (cheddar, Monterey Jack, or your favorite)
- 4 large flour tortillas
- Optional toppings: salsa, guacamole, sour cream, chopped cilantro, diced tomatoes, shredded lettuce, sliced jalapeños

Instructions:

1. In a skillet, heat a little oil over medium heat. Add diced onion and minced garlic, and cook until softened and fragrant, about 3-4 minutes.
2. Add cooked rice, black beans, ground cumin, chili powder, salt, and pepper to the skillet. Stir well to combine and cook for another 2-3 minutes until heated through.
3. Warm the flour tortillas in a dry skillet or microwave for a few seconds to make them pliable.
4. Divide the rice and bean mixture evenly among the tortillas, placing it in the center of each.
5. Sprinkle shredded cheese over the rice and bean mixture on each tortilla.
6. Optional: Add any additional toppings you desire, such as salsa, guacamole, sour cream, chopped cilantro, diced tomatoes, shredded lettuce, or sliced jalapeños.
7. Fold the sides of each tortilla over the filling, then roll them up tightly to form burritos.
8. If desired, you can grill the burritos on a skillet or griddle for a few minutes on each side to crisp them up and melt the cheese.
9. Serve the rice and bean burritos immediately, with additional toppings on the side if desired.

Enjoy your delicious and customizable Rice and Bean Burritos! They're perfect for a quick and satisfying meal any time of day.

Minestrone Soup

Ingredients:

- 2 tablespoons olive oil
- 1 onion, diced
- 2 carrots, diced
- 2 celery stalks, diced
- 3 cloves garlic, minced
- 1 can (14 ounces) diced tomatoes
- 6 cups vegetable broth
- 1 can (15 ounces) kidney beans, drained and rinsed
- 1 can (15 ounces) cannellini beans, drained and rinsed
- 1 cup small pasta (such as ditalini or small shells)
- 2 cups chopped fresh spinach or kale
- 1 teaspoon dried oregano
- 1 teaspoon dried basil
- Salt and pepper, to taste
- Grated Parmesan cheese, for serving (optional)

Instructions:

1. Heat olive oil in a large pot over medium heat. Add diced onion, carrots, and celery. Cook, stirring occasionally, until vegetables are softened, about 5-7 minutes.
2. Add minced garlic to the pot and cook for another minute until fragrant.
3. Stir in diced tomatoes and vegetable broth. Bring the mixture to a simmer.
4. Add drained and rinsed kidney beans and cannellini beans to the pot.
5. Stir in the pasta and continue to simmer until the pasta is cooked according to package instructions, usually about 8-10 minutes.
6. Once the pasta is cooked, stir in chopped spinach or kale and dried oregano and basil. Simmer for another 2-3 minutes until the greens are wilted.
7. Season the soup with salt and pepper to taste.
8. Serve the Minestrone Soup hot, garnished with grated Parmesan cheese if desired.

Enjoy your delicious and comforting Minestrone Soup! It's perfect for a cozy meal on a chilly day.

Mushroom and Spinach Pasta

Ingredients:

- 8 ounces (225g) pasta (such as spaghetti, fettuccine, or penne)
- 2 tablespoons olive oil
- 3 cloves garlic, minced
- 8 ounces (225g) mushrooms, sliced (cremini, button, or your choice)
- 4 cups fresh spinach leaves, washed and chopped
- 1/2 cup grated Parmesan cheese
- Salt and pepper, to taste
- Red pepper flakes (optional)
- Fresh parsley, chopped, for garnish (optional)

Instructions:

1. Cook the pasta according to the package instructions in a large pot of salted boiling water until al dente. Drain and set aside, reserving some pasta water.
2. In a large skillet, heat olive oil over medium heat. Add minced garlic and cook for about 1 minute until fragrant.
3. Add sliced mushrooms to the skillet and cook, stirring occasionally, until they release their moisture and become golden brown, about 5-7 minutes.
4. Stir in chopped spinach leaves and cook until wilted, about 2-3 minutes.
5. Add the cooked pasta to the skillet and toss to combine with the mushroom and spinach mixture.
6. Stir in grated Parmesan cheese and toss until the cheese is melted and the pasta is coated evenly. If the pasta seems dry, add a splash of reserved pasta water to loosen it up.
7. Season with salt, pepper, and red pepper flakes (if using), to taste.
8. Serve the Mushroom and Spinach Pasta hot, garnished with chopped fresh parsley if desired.

Enjoy your delicious and nutritious Mushroom and Spinach Pasta! It's a quick and satisfying meal that's perfect for busy weeknights.

Baked Beans on Toast

Ingredients:

- 1 can (15 ounces) baked beans in tomato sauce
- 4 slices of bread (your choice), toasted
- Butter or margarine, for spreading (optional)
- Salt and pepper, to taste
- Optional toppings: grated cheese, chopped fresh parsley, sliced tomatoes, fried or poached egg

Instructions:

1. Heat the baked beans in a saucepan over medium heat until hot, stirring occasionally.
2. While the beans are heating, toast the bread slices until golden brown.
3. If desired, spread butter or margarine on the toasted bread slices.
4. Spoon the hot baked beans over the toast, dividing them evenly among the slices.
5. Season the beans with salt and pepper to taste.
6. Optional: Sprinkle grated cheese over the hot beans for extra flavor and richness.
7. Serve the baked beans on toast immediately, garnished with chopped fresh parsley if desired.
8. Optional: Top each serving with sliced tomatoes or a fried or poached egg for added protein and flavor.

Enjoy your delicious and satisfying baked beans on toast! It's perfect for breakfast, brunch, or a quick and comforting meal any time of day.

Mexican Rice Casserole

Ingredients:

- 1 cup long-grain white rice
- 1 tablespoon olive oil
- 1 onion, diced
- 2 cloves garlic, minced
- 1 bell pepper, diced
- 1 can (15 ounces) black beans, drained and rinsed
- 1 cup corn kernels (fresh, frozen, or canned)
- 1 can (14.5 ounces) diced tomatoes
- 1 cup salsa
- 1 cup vegetable broth or water
- 1 teaspoon chili powder
- 1 teaspoon ground cumin
- 1/2 teaspoon smoked paprika
- Salt and pepper, to taste
- 1 cup shredded cheese (cheddar, Monterey Jack, or your favorite)
- Optional toppings: chopped fresh cilantro, sliced green onions, diced avocado, sour cream

Instructions:

1. Preheat your oven to 375°F (190°C). Lightly grease a 9x13-inch baking dish.
2. In a large skillet, heat olive oil over medium heat. Add diced onion and cook until softened, about 5 minutes.
3. Add minced garlic and diced bell pepper to the skillet and cook for another 2-3 minutes until fragrant.
4. Stir in long-grain white rice and cook for 1-2 minutes until lightly toasted.
5. Add drained and rinsed black beans, corn kernels, diced tomatoes, salsa, vegetable broth or water, chili powder, ground cumin, smoked paprika, salt, and pepper to the skillet. Stir well to combine.
6. Bring the mixture to a simmer, then reduce the heat to low. Cover and cook for about 15-20 minutes, or until the rice is cooked and most of the liquid is absorbed.
7. Transfer the rice mixture to the prepared baking dish and spread it out evenly.
8. Sprinkle shredded cheese over the top of the rice mixture.
9. Cover the baking dish with aluminum foil and bake in the preheated oven for 20-25 minutes, or until the cheese is melted and bubbly.
10. Remove the foil and bake for an additional 5-10 minutes, or until the cheese is golden brown and bubbly.
11. Remove the casserole from the oven and let it cool for a few minutes before serving.

12. Serve the Mexican Rice Casserole hot, garnished with optional toppings such as chopped fresh cilantro, sliced green onions, diced avocado, and sour cream.

Enjoy your delicious and flavorful Mexican Rice Casserole! It's perfect for a comforting dinner or for feeding a crowd at potlucks and gatherings.

Sweet Potato and Black Bean Enchiladas

Ingredients:

For the filling:

- 2 medium sweet potatoes, peeled and diced into small cubes
- 1 can (15 ounces) black beans, drained and rinsed
- 1 onion, diced
- 2 cloves garlic, minced
- 1 teaspoon ground cumin
- 1 teaspoon chili powder
- 1/2 teaspoon paprika
- Salt and pepper, to taste
- 1 tablespoon olive oil

For the enchilada sauce:

- 2 tablespoons olive oil
- 2 tablespoons all-purpose flour
- 2 tablespoons chili powder
- 1 teaspoon ground cumin
- 1 teaspoon garlic powder
- 1/2 teaspoon dried oregano
- 2 cups vegetable broth
- 1 can (8 ounces) tomato sauce
- Salt and pepper, to taste

For assembling:

- 8-10 large flour tortillas
- 1 1/2 cups shredded cheese (cheddar, Monterey Jack, or your favorite)
- Optional toppings: chopped cilantro, diced avocado, sour cream, sliced jalapeños

Instructions:

1. Preheat your oven to 375°F (190°C).

2. In a large skillet, heat 1 tablespoon of olive oil over medium heat. Add diced sweet potatoes and cook until tender, about 10-12 minutes.
3. Add diced onion and minced garlic to the skillet and cook for another 2-3 minutes until softened.
4. Stir in drained and rinsed black beans, ground cumin, chili powder, paprika, salt, and pepper. Cook for an additional 2-3 minutes until the flavors are well combined. Remove from heat and set aside.
5. In a separate saucepan, heat 2 tablespoons of olive oil over medium heat. Whisk in all-purpose flour and cook for 1-2 minutes until lightly browned and fragrant.
6. Stir in chili powder, ground cumin, garlic powder, and dried oregano. Cook for another minute.
7. Gradually whisk in vegetable broth and tomato sauce until smooth. Bring the mixture to a simmer and cook for 5-7 minutes until thickened. Season with salt and pepper to taste.
8. Spread a thin layer of enchilada sauce on the bottom of a 9x13-inch baking dish.
9. Spoon the sweet potato and black bean mixture into each flour tortilla, roll them up, and place them seam-side down in the baking dish.
10. Pour the remaining enchilada sauce over the top of the rolled tortillas, spreading it out evenly.
11. Sprinkle shredded cheese over the top of the enchiladas.
12. Cover the baking dish with aluminum foil and bake in the preheated oven for 20-25 minutes, or until the cheese is melted and bubbly.
13. Remove the foil and bake for an additional 5 minutes, or until the cheese is golden brown and bubbly.
14. Remove the enchiladas from the oven and let them cool for a few minutes before serving.
15. Serve the Sweet Potato and Black Bean Enchiladas hot, garnished with optional toppings such as chopped cilantro, diced avocado, sour cream, and sliced jalapeños.

Enjoy your delicious and satisfying Sweet Potato and Black Bean Enchiladas! They're perfect for a flavorful and nutritious meal.

Ratatouille

Ingredients:

- 1 large eggplant, diced
- 2 medium zucchini, diced
- 1 large onion, diced
- 2 bell peppers (red, yellow, or green), diced
- 4 cloves garlic, minced
- 4 tomatoes, diced (or 1 can of diced tomatoes)
- 2 tablespoons tomato paste
- 2 tablespoons olive oil
- 1 teaspoon dried thyme
- 1 teaspoon dried oregano
- Salt and pepper, to taste
- Fresh basil leaves, chopped, for garnish (optional)

Instructions:

1. Heat olive oil in a large skillet or Dutch oven over medium heat. Add diced onion and minced garlic, and cook until softened and fragrant, about 5 minutes.
2. Add diced eggplant, zucchini, and bell peppers to the skillet. Cook, stirring occasionally, until the vegetables start to soften, about 10 minutes.
3. Stir in diced tomatoes, tomato paste, dried thyme, dried oregano, salt, and pepper. Mix well to combine.
4. Reduce the heat to low, cover the skillet, and let the ratatouille simmer gently for about 20-30 minutes, stirring occasionally, until the vegetables are tender and the flavors have melded together.
5. Taste and adjust seasoning if needed.
6. Serve the ratatouille hot, garnished with chopped fresh basil leaves if desired.

Enjoy your delicious and vibrant Ratatouille! It's perfect as a side dish, main course, or served over rice or pasta for a complete meal.

Broccoli and Cheddar Quesadillas

Ingredients:

- 2 cups broccoli florets, chopped into small pieces
- 1 tablespoon olive oil
- 1/2 teaspoon garlic powder
- Salt and pepper, to taste
- 4 large flour tortillas
- 2 cups shredded cheddar cheese
- Optional toppings: salsa, sour cream, guacamole, chopped cilantro

Instructions:

1. Preheat your oven to 400°F (200°C).
2. In a large skillet, heat olive oil over medium heat. Add chopped broccoli florets, garlic powder, salt, and pepper. Cook, stirring occasionally, for about 5-7 minutes until the broccoli is tender-crisp. Remove from heat and set aside.
3. Place two flour tortillas on a baking sheet. Sprinkle shredded cheddar cheese evenly over each tortilla.
4. Divide the cooked broccoli evenly between the two tortillas, spreading it out over one half of each tortilla.
5. Fold the other half of each tortilla over the broccoli and cheese to form a half-moon shape.
6. Bake the quesadillas in the preheated oven for about 5-7 minutes, or until the cheese is melted and the tortillas are golden brown and crispy.
7. Remove the quesadillas from the oven and let them cool for a minute or two before slicing into wedges.
8. Serve the Broccoli and Cheddar Quesadillas hot, with optional toppings such as salsa, sour cream, guacamole, or chopped cilantro on the side.

Enjoy your delicious and cheesy Broccoli and Cheddar Quesadillas! They're perfect for a quick and satisfying meal or snack.

Peanut Noodles

Ingredients:

For the sauce:

- 1/4 cup creamy peanut butter
- 3 tablespoons soy sauce
- 2 tablespoons rice vinegar
- 1 tablespoon sesame oil
- 1 tablespoon honey or maple syrup
- 1 clove garlic, minced
- 1 teaspoon grated fresh ginger
- Pinch of red pepper flakes (optional)
- 2-4 tablespoons water, as needed to thin the sauce

For the noodles:

- 8 ounces (about 225g) noodles of your choice (such as spaghetti, linguine, or rice noodles)
- 1 tablespoon sesame oil (for tossing noodles)
- Optional toppings: chopped green onions, chopped peanuts, sesame seeds, sliced cucumber, shredded carrots, chopped cilantro

Instructions:

1. Cook the noodles according to the package instructions until al dente. Drain and rinse under cold water to stop the cooking process. Toss the cooked noodles with 1 tablespoon of sesame oil to prevent sticking.
2. In a medium bowl, whisk together creamy peanut butter, soy sauce, rice vinegar, sesame oil, honey or maple syrup, minced garlic, grated fresh ginger, and a pinch of red pepper flakes until smooth. If the sauce is too thick, add water, 1 tablespoon at a time, until desired consistency is reached.
3. Pour the peanut sauce over the cooked and cooled noodles. Toss until the noodles are evenly coated with the sauce.
4. Serve the peanut noodles immediately, garnished with your choice of toppings such as chopped green onions, chopped peanuts, sesame seeds, sliced cucumber, shredded carrots, and chopped cilantro.

5. Enjoy your delicious Peanut Noodles as a main dish or side dish! They can be served warm, at room temperature, or chilled, making them perfect for picnics, potlucks, or meal prep.

Lentil Tacos

Ingredients:

For the lentil filling:

- 1 cup dry brown or green lentils
- 2 cups vegetable broth or water
- 1 tablespoon olive oil
- 1 onion, diced
- 2 cloves garlic, minced
- 1 bell pepper, diced
- 1 tablespoon chili powder
- 1 teaspoon ground cumin
- 1 teaspoon paprika
- 1/2 teaspoon dried oregano
- Salt and pepper, to taste

For serving:

- Hard or soft taco shells
- Shredded lettuce
- Diced tomatoes
- Diced avocado or guacamole
- Shredded cheese
- Sour cream or Greek yogurt
- Salsa
- Chopped cilantro
- Lime wedges

Instructions:

1. Rinse the lentils under cold water. In a medium saucepan, bring the vegetable broth or water to a boil. Add the lentils, reduce the heat to low, cover, and simmer for 20-25 minutes, or until the lentils are tender but not mushy. Drain any excess liquid and set aside.

2. In a large skillet, heat the olive oil over medium heat. Add the diced onion and cook until softened, about 5 minutes.
3. Add the minced garlic and diced bell pepper to the skillet and cook for another 2-3 minutes until fragrant.
4. Add the cooked lentils to the skillet, along with the chili powder, ground cumin, paprika, dried oregano, salt, and pepper. Stir well to combine and cook for another 5-7 minutes, stirring occasionally, until heated through and the flavors are well blended.
5. Taste and adjust seasoning if needed.
6. Serve the lentil filling warm in taco shells, topped with your choice of toppings such as shredded lettuce, diced tomatoes, diced avocado or guacamole, shredded cheese, sour cream or Greek yogurt, salsa, chopped cilantro, and lime wedges.
7. Enjoy your delicious and satisfying Lentil Tacos! They're perfect for a quick and healthy weeknight dinner or for entertaining guests.

Tomato and Mozzarella Panini

Ingredients:

- 4 slices of bread (such as ciabatta, focaccia, or sourdough)
- 2 large tomatoes, thinly sliced
- 1 ball of fresh mozzarella cheese, thinly sliced
- Fresh basil leaves
- Olive oil, for brushing
- Salt and pepper, to taste

Instructions:

1. Preheat a panini press or a skillet over medium heat.
2. Place the bread slices on a clean surface. Layer the tomato slices, mozzarella slices, and fresh basil leaves on two slices of bread. Season with salt and pepper to taste.
3. Top each sandwich with the remaining slices of bread to form two sandwiches.
4. Brush the outsides of the sandwiches lightly with olive oil.
5. Place the sandwiches on the preheated panini press or skillet. If using a skillet, you can place a heavy pan or a foil-wrapped brick on top of the sandwiches to press them down.
6. Cook the sandwiches for 3-5 minutes on each side, or until the bread is golden brown and the cheese is melted.
7. Remove the sandwiches from the panini press or skillet and let them cool slightly before slicing them in half.
8. Serve the Tomato and Mozzarella Panini warm, and enjoy the gooey cheese and flavorful tomatoes with the crispy bread!

These paninis are perfect for a quick lunch or dinner and can be customized with your favorite ingredients or additions like pesto, spinach, or roasted red peppers.

Creamy Mushroom Pasta

Ingredients:

- 8 ounces (225g) pasta of your choice (such as fettuccine, linguine, or penne)
- 2 tablespoons butter
- 2 tablespoons olive oil
- 1 pound (450g) mushrooms (such as cremini or button), sliced
- 3 cloves garlic, minced
- 1 cup (240ml) chicken or vegetable broth
- 1 cup (240ml) heavy cream
- 1/2 cup (120ml) grated Parmesan cheese
- Salt and pepper, to taste
- Fresh parsley, chopped, for garnish (optional)

Instructions:

1. Cook the pasta according to the package instructions until al dente. Drain and set aside, reserving some pasta water.
2. In a large skillet, heat the butter and olive oil over medium heat. Add the sliced mushrooms and cook, stirring occasionally, until they are golden brown and tender, about 8-10 minutes.
3. Add the minced garlic to the skillet and cook for another minute until fragrant.
4. Pour in the chicken or vegetable broth and bring it to a simmer. Let it cook for a few minutes until slightly reduced.
5. Stir in the heavy cream and grated Parmesan cheese. Season with salt and pepper to taste. Simmer the sauce for a few more minutes until it thickens slightly.
6. Add the cooked pasta to the skillet and toss to coat it evenly with the creamy mushroom sauce. If the sauce is too thick, you can add a splash of reserved pasta water to thin it out.
7. Serve the creamy mushroom pasta hot, garnished with chopped fresh parsley if desired.
8. Enjoy your delicious and creamy mushroom pasta as a comforting and satisfying meal!

Feel free to customize this recipe by adding cooked chicken, bacon, spinach, or any other ingredients you like. It's versatile and adaptable to your preferences.

Corn and Black Bean Salad

Ingredients:

- 2 cups cooked corn kernels (fresh, frozen, or canned)
- 1 can (15 ounces) black beans, drained and rinsed
- 1 red bell pepper, diced
- 1/2 red onion, finely chopped
- 1/4 cup chopped fresh cilantro
- Juice of 2 limes
- 2 tablespoons olive oil
- 1 teaspoon ground cumin
- Salt and pepper to taste
- Optional: diced avocado, cherry tomatoes, jalapeño peppers for extra flavor and heat

Instructions:

1. Prepare the Ingredients: Cook the corn kernels if using fresh or frozen corn. If using canned corn, drain well. Drain and rinse the black beans. Dice the red bell pepper, finely chop the red onion, and chop the cilantro.
2. Combine Ingredients: In a large mixing bowl, combine the cooked corn, black beans, diced red bell pepper, chopped red onion, and chopped cilantro.
3. Make the Dressing: In a small bowl, whisk together the lime juice, olive oil, ground cumin, salt, and pepper.
4. Toss the Salad: Pour the dressing over the corn and black bean mixture in the large bowl. Gently toss until all ingredients are evenly coated with the dressing.
5. Chill and Serve: Cover the salad and refrigerate for at least 30 minutes to allow the flavors to meld together. Before serving, taste and adjust seasoning if necessary. If desired, garnish with diced avocado, cherry tomatoes, or jalapeño peppers.
6. Serve: Serve chilled as a side dish or a light main course. Enjoy!

This salad is not only delicious but also versatile. You can customize it by adding other ingredients like diced avocado, cherry tomatoes, or jalapeños to suit your taste preferences. It's a great dish to bring to potlucks or serve at gatherings because it's colorful, healthy, and full of flavor!

Eggplant Parmesan

Ingredients:

- 2 large eggplants, sliced into 1/2-inch rounds
- 2 cups breadcrumbs (preferably Italian-style)
- 1 cup grated Parmesan cheese
- 4 large eggs, beaten
- Salt and pepper to taste
- Olive oil for frying
- 4 cups marinara sauce (homemade or store-bought)
- 2 cups shredded mozzarella cheese
- Fresh basil leaves for garnish (optional)

Instructions:

1. Prepare the Eggplant: Sprinkle the eggplant slices with salt and let them sit in a colander for about 30 minutes. This helps to draw out excess moisture and bitterness from the eggplant. After 30 minutes, rinse the eggplant slices and pat them dry with paper towels.
2. Bread the Eggplant: In a shallow dish, combine the breadcrumbs with half of the grated Parmesan cheese. In another shallow dish, beat the eggs with a pinch of salt and pepper. Dip each eggplant slice into the beaten eggs, allowing any excess to drip off, then coat it in the breadcrumb mixture, pressing gently to adhere. Place the breaded eggplant slices on a baking sheet lined with parchment paper.
3. Fry the Eggplant: In a large skillet, heat about 1/4 inch of olive oil over medium heat. Working in batches, fry the breaded eggplant slices until golden brown and crispy on both sides, about 2-3 minutes per side. Transfer the fried eggplant slices to a plate lined with paper towels to drain any excess oil.
4. Assemble the Dish: Preheat the oven to 375°F (190°C). Spread a thin layer of marinara sauce on the bottom of a 9x13-inch baking dish. Arrange a single layer of fried eggplant slices on top of the sauce. Spoon more marinara sauce over the eggplant slices, then sprinkle with shredded mozzarella cheese and the remaining grated Parmesan cheese. Repeat the layers until all the eggplant slices are used, finishing with a layer of marinara sauce and cheese on top.
5. Bake: Cover the baking dish with aluminum foil and bake in the preheated oven for 25-30 minutes, or until the cheese is melted and bubbly.
6. Serve: Remove the foil from the baking dish and let the Eggplant Parmesan cool for a few minutes before serving. Garnish with fresh basil leaves if desired. Serve hot and enjoy!

Eggplant Parmesan pairs well with a side of pasta or a crisp green salad for a satisfying meal.

It's a comforting dish that's sure to please both vegetarians and meat-eaters alike!

Veggie Pad Thai

Ingredients:

- 8 ounces flat rice noodles
- 2 tablespoons vegetable oil
- 2 cloves garlic, minced
- 1 small onion, thinly sliced
- 1 red bell pepper, julienned
- 1 carrot, julienned
- 1 cup broccoli florets
- 1 cup sliced mushrooms
- 1 cup firm tofu, cubed
- 2 eggs, lightly beaten (optional, omit for vegan version)
- 1/4 cup chopped peanuts, for garnish
- 2 green onions, chopped, for garnish
- Lime wedges, for serving

For the sauce:

- 3 tablespoons soy sauce
- 2 tablespoons tamarind paste
- 2 tablespoons brown sugar
- 1 tablespoon rice vinegar
- 1 tablespoon Sriracha sauce (adjust to taste)
- 1 teaspoon minced ginger
- 1 teaspoon minced lemongrass (optional)

Instructions:

1. Prepare the Rice Noodles: Cook the rice noodles according to the package instructions until they are al dente. Drain and rinse with cold water to stop the cooking process. Set aside.
2. Make the Sauce: In a small bowl, whisk together the soy sauce, tamarind paste, brown sugar, rice vinegar, Sriracha sauce, minced ginger, and minced lemongrass until well combined. Adjust the seasoning to taste.
3. Stir-Fry the Vegetables and Tofu: Heat the vegetable oil in a large skillet or wok over medium-high heat. Add the minced garlic and sliced onion, and stir-fry for about 1 minute until fragrant. Add the julienned red bell pepper, carrot, broccoli florets, and sliced mushrooms. Stir-fry for another 3-4 minutes until the vegetables are tender-crisp.
4. Add Tofu and Eggs: Push the vegetables to one side of the skillet or wok and add the cubed tofu to the empty space. Cook for 2-3 minutes until the tofu starts to brown slightly. If using eggs, push the tofu to the side and pour the beaten eggs into the empty

space. Allow the eggs to set slightly, then scramble them with a spatula until cooked through.
5. Combine Everything: Add the cooked rice noodles to the skillet or wok along with the prepared sauce. Toss everything together until the noodles are well coated in the sauce and heated through.
6. Serve: Transfer the Veggie Pad Thai to serving plates or bowls. Garnish with chopped peanuts and green onions. Serve with lime wedges on the side for squeezing over the noodles.

Enjoy your homemade Veggie Pad Thai as a satisfying and flavorful meal that's packed with vibrant vegetables and bold Thai flavors!

BBQ Chickpea Wraps

Ingredients:

For the BBQ Chickpeas:

- 2 cans (15 ounces each) chickpeas, drained and rinsed
- 1 cup BBQ sauce
- 2 tablespoons olive oil
- 1 teaspoon smoked paprika
- 1 teaspoon garlic powder
- Salt and pepper to taste

For the Wraps:

- 4 large whole wheat or spinach tortillas
- 1 cup shredded lettuce or mixed greens
- 1 cup diced tomatoes
- 1/2 cup diced red onion
- 1 avocado, sliced
- 1/2 cup shredded cheese (optional, omit for vegan version)
- Ranch dressing or vegan mayo for drizzling (optional)
- Fresh cilantro or parsley for garnish (optional)

Instructions:

1. Prepare the BBQ Chickpeas: Preheat your oven to 400°F (200°C). In a mixing bowl, combine the drained and rinsed chickpeas with BBQ sauce, olive oil, smoked paprika, garlic powder, salt, and pepper. Toss until the chickpeas are well coated.
2. Roast the Chickpeas: Spread the seasoned chickpeas in a single layer on a baking sheet lined with parchment paper. Roast in the preheated oven for 20-25 minutes, stirring halfway through, until the chickpeas are crispy and caramelized.
3. Assemble the Wraps: Lay out the tortillas on a flat surface. Place a portion of shredded lettuce or mixed greens in the center of each tortilla. Top with a generous spoonful of BBQ chickpeas, diced tomatoes, diced red onion, avocado slices, and shredded cheese (if using).
4. Drizzle with Dressing: Drizzle ranch dressing or vegan mayo over the filling ingredients, if desired, for added flavor.
5. Fold and Serve: Fold the bottom edge of each tortilla up over the filling, then fold in the sides, and roll tightly to form a wrap. Secure with toothpicks if needed. Repeat with the remaining tortillas and filling ingredients.
6. Garnish and Serve: Garnish the BBQ Chickpea Wraps with fresh cilantro or parsley, if desired. Serve immediately, or wrap each wrap in parchment paper or foil for easy transport or storage.

These BBQ Chickpea Wraps are perfect for a quick and satisfying lunch or dinner. They're customizable, so feel free to add or substitute your favorite veggies and toppings to suit your taste preferences. Enjoy!

Spinach and Ricotta Stuffed Shells

Ingredients:

- 1 box (12 ounces) jumbo pasta shells
- 2 cups ricotta cheese
- 1 cup grated Parmesan cheese, divided
- 1 large egg
- 2 cups chopped spinach (fresh or frozen, thawed and drained)
- 2 cloves garlic, minced
- 1 teaspoon dried basil
- 1 teaspoon dried oregano
- Salt and pepper to taste
- 2 cups marinara sauce
- 1 cup shredded mozzarella cheese
- Fresh basil leaves, chopped, for garnish (optional)

Instructions:

1. Cook the Pasta Shells: Bring a large pot of salted water to a boil. Cook the jumbo pasta shells according to the package instructions until al dente. Drain the shells and rinse them under cold water to stop the cooking process. Set aside.
2. Prepare the Filling: In a large mixing bowl, combine the ricotta cheese, 1/2 cup of grated Parmesan cheese, egg, chopped spinach, minced garlic, dried basil, dried oregano, salt, and pepper. Mix well until all ingredients are evenly combined.
3. Stuff the Shells: Preheat your oven to 375°F (190°C). Spread a thin layer of marinara sauce on the bottom of a 9x13-inch baking dish. Using a spoon, carefully stuff each cooked pasta shell with the spinach and ricotta mixture, and place them in the baking dish.
4. Top with Sauce and Cheese: Once all the shells are stuffed and arranged in the baking dish, spoon the remaining marinara sauce over the top, covering the shells evenly. Sprinkle the shredded mozzarella cheese and the remaining 1/2 cup of grated Parmesan cheese over the sauce.
5. Bake: Cover the baking dish with aluminum foil and bake in the preheated oven for 25-30 minutes, or until the cheese is melted and bubbly.
6. Serve: Remove the foil from the baking dish and let the stuffed shells cool for a few minutes before serving. Garnish with chopped fresh basil leaves, if desired. Serve hot and enjoy!

These spinach and ricotta stuffed shells are delicious served on their own or with a side of garlic bread and a green salad. They're a comforting and satisfying meal that's sure to please everyone at the table!

Black Bean and Corn Quesadillas

Ingredients:

- 1 can (15 ounces) black beans, drained and rinsed
- 1 cup corn kernels (fresh, frozen, or canned)
- 1 cup shredded cheese (cheddar, Monterey Jack, or a Mexican blend)
- 1/2 cup diced red bell pepper
- 1/4 cup chopped fresh cilantro
- 1 teaspoon ground cumin
- 1/2 teaspoon chili powder
- Salt and pepper to taste
- 4 large flour tortillas
- Cooking spray or vegetable oil, for cooking
- Optional toppings: salsa, sour cream, guacamole, chopped green onions

Instructions:

1. Prepare the Filling: In a mixing bowl, combine the black beans, corn kernels, shredded cheese, diced red bell pepper, chopped cilantro, ground cumin, chili powder, salt, and pepper. Mix well until all ingredients are evenly distributed.
2. Assemble the Quesadillas: Lay out the flour tortillas on a flat surface. Spoon a portion of the black bean and corn mixture onto one half of each tortilla, spreading it out evenly. Fold the other half of the tortilla over the filling to create a half-moon shape.
3. Cook the Quesadillas: Heat a large skillet or griddle over medium heat. Lightly spray the skillet or brush it with vegetable oil. Place the assembled quesadillas in the skillet and cook for 2-3 minutes on each side, or until golden brown and crispy, and the cheese is melted inside. You may need to cook them in batches depending on the size of your skillet.
4. Serve: Remove the cooked quesadillas from the skillet and let them cool for a minute before slicing them into wedges. Serve hot with your favorite toppings such as salsa, sour cream, guacamole, or chopped green onions.
5. Enjoy! These black bean and corn quesadillas are delicious as a quick and satisfying meal or as a snack for parties or gatherings. They're versatile, so feel free to customize them with additional ingredients like diced jalapeños, diced tomatoes, or sliced avocado.

Veggie Lo Mein

Ingredients:

- 8 ounces lo mein noodles or spaghetti
- 2 tablespoons sesame oil, divided
- 2 cloves garlic, minced
- 1 teaspoon grated ginger
- 1 bell pepper, thinly sliced
- 1 carrot, julienned
- 1 cup snow peas, trimmed
- 1 cup sliced mushrooms
- 2 cups shredded cabbage or coleslaw mix
- 1/4 cup soy sauce
- 2 tablespoons hoisin sauce
- 1 tablespoon rice vinegar
- 1 teaspoon Sriracha sauce (optional, for heat)
- 2 green onions, sliced
- Sesame seeds, for garnish (optional)

Instructions:

1. Cook the Noodles: Bring a large pot of salted water to a boil. Cook the lo mein noodles according to the package instructions until al dente. Drain the noodles and rinse them under cold water to stop the cooking process. Toss the noodles with 1 tablespoon of sesame oil to prevent sticking, and set aside.
2. Prepare the Sauce: In a small bowl, whisk together the soy sauce, hoisin sauce, rice vinegar, and Sriracha sauce (if using). Set the sauce aside.
3. Stir-Fry the Vegetables: Heat the remaining tablespoon of sesame oil in a large skillet or wok over medium-high heat. Add the minced garlic and grated ginger, and stir-fry for about 30 seconds until fragrant. Add the sliced bell pepper, julienned carrot, snow peas, sliced mushrooms, and shredded cabbage to the skillet. Stir-fry for 3-4 minutes until the vegetables are tender-crisp.
4. Combine Everything: Add the cooked lo mein noodles to the skillet with the stir-fried vegetables. Pour the prepared sauce over the noodles and vegetables, and toss everything together until well combined. Cook for an additional 2-3 minutes until heated through.
5. Garnish and Serve: Garnish the veggie lo mein with sliced green onions and sesame seeds, if desired. Serve hot and enjoy!

This veggie lo mein is versatile, so feel free to customize it with your favorite vegetables such as broccoli, bok choy, or snap peas. You can also add tofu, chicken, shrimp, or beef for extra protein if desired. It's a delicious and satisfying dish that's sure to become a favorite in your recipe rotation!

Potato and Chickpea Curry

Ingredients:

- 2 tablespoons vegetable oil
- 1 large onion, finely chopped
- 3 cloves garlic, minced
- 1 tablespoon grated ginger
- 2 large potatoes, peeled and diced
- 1 can (15 ounces) chickpeas, drained and rinsed
- 1 can (14 ounces) diced tomatoes
- 1 can (14 ounces) coconut milk
- 1 tablespoon curry powder
- 1 teaspoon ground cumin
- 1 teaspoon ground coriander
- 1/2 teaspoon turmeric powder
- 1/4 teaspoon cayenne pepper (optional, for heat)
- Salt and pepper to taste
- Fresh cilantro leaves, chopped, for garnish
- Cooked rice or naan bread, for serving

Instructions:

1. Sauté Aromatics: Heat the vegetable oil in a large skillet or pot over medium heat. Add the chopped onion and cook for 5-6 minutes until softened and translucent. Stir in the minced garlic and grated ginger, and cook for an additional 1-2 minutes until fragrant.
2. Add Potatoes: Add the diced potatoes to the skillet, and stir to coat them in the onion mixture. Cook for 5 minutes, stirring occasionally, until the potatoes start to brown slightly.
3. Add Chickpeas and Spices: Stir in the drained and rinsed chickpeas, diced tomatoes, coconut milk, curry powder, ground cumin, ground coriander, turmeric powder, cayenne pepper (if using), salt, and pepper. Mix well to combine all the ingredients.
4. Simmer: Bring the mixture to a simmer, then reduce the heat to low. Cover the skillet or pot with a lid and let the curry simmer for 20-25 minutes, stirring occasionally, until the potatoes are tender and the flavors have melded together.
5. Adjust Seasoning: Taste the curry and adjust the seasoning if necessary, adding more salt, pepper, or spices according to your preference.
6. Serve: Once the potatoes are cooked through and the curry has reached your desired consistency, remove the skillet or pot from the heat. Garnish the potato and chickpea curry with chopped fresh cilantro leaves. Serve hot with cooked rice or naan bread.

This potato and chickpea curry is rich, creamy, and full of aromatic spices. It's a delicious vegetarian dish that's perfect for a cozy dinner at home. Enjoy!

Greek Quinoa Salad

Ingredients:

- 1 cup quinoa
- 2 cups water or vegetable broth
- 1 cup cherry tomatoes, halved
- 1 cucumber, diced
- 1/2 red onion, thinly sliced
- 1/2 cup Kalamata olives, pitted and halved
- 1/2 cup crumbled feta cheese
- 1/4 cup chopped fresh parsley
- 1/4 cup chopped fresh mint
- Juice of 1-2 lemons
- 3 tablespoons extra virgin olive oil
- 1 teaspoon dried oregano
- Salt and pepper to taste

Instructions:

1. Cook the Quinoa: Rinse the quinoa under cold water using a fine mesh sieve. In a saucepan, combine the rinsed quinoa and water or vegetable broth. Bring to a boil, then reduce the heat to low, cover, and simmer for 15-20 minutes, or until the quinoa is cooked and the liquid is absorbed. Remove from heat and let it cool.
2. Prepare the Vegetables: In a large mixing bowl, combine the halved cherry tomatoes, diced cucumber, thinly sliced red onion, halved Kalamata olives, crumbled feta cheese, chopped fresh parsley, and chopped fresh mint.
3. Make the Dressing: In a small bowl, whisk together the lemon juice, extra virgin olive oil, dried oregano, salt, and pepper until well combined.
4. Combine Everything: Add the cooked and cooled quinoa to the bowl of vegetables and herbs. Pour the dressing over the quinoa and vegetables, and toss everything together until well coated.
5. Chill and Serve: Cover the bowl with plastic wrap or transfer the salad to a container with a lid. Refrigerate for at least 30 minutes to allow the flavors to meld together.
6. Serve: Once chilled, give the Greek quinoa salad a final toss, taste and adjust seasoning if needed, and serve. Enjoy as a light and refreshing meal or as a side dish to grilled meats or fish.

This Greek quinoa salad is not only delicious but also versatile and nutritious. It's perfect for meal prep, picnics, potlucks, or as a healthy lunch option. Feel free to customize it by adding other ingredients like bell peppers, artichoke hearts, or avocado according to your taste preferences.

Spinach and Mushroom Quiche

Ingredients:

For the Crust:

- 1 1/4 cups all-purpose flour
- 1/2 teaspoon salt
- 1/2 cup cold unsalted butter, diced
- 1/4 cup ice water

For the Filling:

- 1 tablespoon olive oil
- 1 small onion, finely chopped
- 8 ounces mushrooms, sliced
- 2 cups fresh spinach leaves, chopped
- 4 large eggs
- 1 cup milk (whole or 2%)
- 1 cup shredded cheese (such as Swiss, Gruyere, or cheddar)
- Salt and pepper to taste
- Pinch of nutmeg (optional)
- Fresh herbs for garnish (such as parsley or chives)

Instructions:

For the Crust:

1. Prepare the Dough: In a large mixing bowl, combine the all-purpose flour and salt. Add the diced cold butter and use a pastry cutter or your fingers to work the butter into the flour until the mixture resembles coarse crumbs.
2. Add Water: Gradually add the ice water, a tablespoon at a time, mixing with a fork until the dough comes together. Be careful not to overwork the dough. Shape the dough into a disk, wrap it in plastic wrap, and refrigerate for at least 30 minutes.
3. Roll Out the Dough: Preheat your oven to 375°F (190°C). On a lightly floured surface, roll out the chilled dough into a circle large enough to fit into a 9-inch pie dish. Carefully transfer the dough to the pie dish, pressing it gently into the bottom and up the sides. Trim any excess dough and crimp the edges. Prick the bottom of the crust with a fork to prevent it from puffing up during baking.
4. Pre-Bake the Crust: Line the crust with parchment paper or aluminum foil and fill it with pie weights or dried beans. Bake in the preheated oven for 15 minutes. Remove the

weights and parchment paper or foil, and bake for an additional 5 minutes until the crust is golden brown. Remove from the oven and set aside.

For the Filling:

1. Prepare the Vegetables: In a skillet, heat the olive oil over medium heat. Add the finely chopped onion and cook for 2-3 minutes until softened. Add the sliced mushrooms and cook for 5-7 minutes until they are golden brown and any liquid released has evaporated. Add the chopped spinach and cook for an additional 2 minutes until wilted. Remove from heat and let the mixture cool slightly.
2. Prepare the Custard: In a mixing bowl, whisk together the eggs, milk, shredded cheese, salt, pepper, and pinch of nutmeg (if using) until well combined.
3. Assemble the Quiche: Spread the cooked mushroom and spinach mixture evenly over the pre-baked crust. Pour the egg and cheese mixture over the vegetables, ensuring that it is evenly distributed.
4. Bake: Place the quiche in the preheated oven and bake for 30-35 minutes, or until the filling is set and the top is golden brown.
5. Serve: Remove the quiche from the oven and let it cool for a few minutes before slicing. Garnish with fresh herbs, if desired. Serve warm or at room temperature.

This spinach and mushroom quiche is delicious served on its own or with a side salad for a complete meal. It's versatile, so feel free to customize it by adding other ingredients such as sun-dried tomatoes, bell peppers, or different types of cheese. Enjoy!

Veggie Fajitas

Ingredients:

For the Fajita Seasoning:

- 1 tablespoon chili powder
- 1 teaspoon ground cumin
- 1 teaspoon smoked paprika
- 1/2 teaspoon garlic powder
- 1/2 teaspoon onion powder
- 1/4 teaspoon cayenne pepper (adjust to taste)
- Salt and pepper to taste

For the Veggie Fajitas:

- 2 tablespoons vegetable oil
- 1 onion, sliced
- 1 red bell pepper, sliced
- 1 green bell pepper, sliced
- 1 yellow or orange bell pepper, sliced
- 1 zucchini, sliced
- 1 yellow squash, sliced
- 8-10 button mushrooms, sliced
- Fajita seasoning (from above)
- Juice of 1 lime
- 8-10 small flour tortillas
- Optional toppings: sliced avocado, chopped cilantro, sour cream or Greek yogurt, salsa, shredded cheese

Instructions:

1. Prepare the Fajita Seasoning: In a small bowl, combine the chili powder, ground cumin, smoked paprika, garlic powder, onion powder, cayenne pepper, salt, and pepper. Mix well to combine.
2. Cook the Veggies: Heat one tablespoon of vegetable oil in a large skillet or wok over medium-high heat. Add the sliced onion and bell peppers to the skillet and cook, stirring occasionally, for 3-4 minutes until they start to soften. Add the sliced zucchini, yellow squash, and mushrooms to the skillet and continue to cook for an additional 4-5 minutes until all the vegetables are tender-crisp.
3. Season the Veggies: Sprinkle the fajita seasoning over the cooked vegetables and squeeze the lime juice over the top. Toss everything together until the vegetables are evenly coated with the seasoning.

4. Warm the Tortillas: While the veggies are cooking, warm the flour tortillas. You can do this by wrapping them in aluminum foil and placing them in a preheated oven at 350°F (175°C) for 5-7 minutes, or by heating them on a dry skillet over medium heat for 30 seconds on each side.
5. Assemble the Fajitas: Spoon the cooked veggie mixture onto the warm flour tortillas. Add any desired toppings such as sliced avocado, chopped cilantro, sour cream or Greek yogurt, salsa, and shredded cheese.
6. Serve: Roll up the tortillas and serve the veggie fajitas immediately. Enjoy!

These veggie fajitas are versatile, so feel free to customize them with your favorite vegetables and toppings. They're a delicious and healthy option for a meatless meal that's full of flavor!

Spicy Peanut Butter Noodles

Ingredients:

- 8 ounces spaghetti or noodles of your choice
- 1/3 cup creamy peanut butter
- 3 tablespoons soy sauce
- 2 tablespoons rice vinegar
- 1 tablespoon sesame oil
- 2 teaspoons Sriracha sauce (adjust to taste)
- 2 cloves garlic, minced
- 1 teaspoon grated ginger
- 1 tablespoon honey or maple syrup
- Juice of 1 lime
- 1/4 cup water (or more as needed)
- 2 green onions, thinly sliced
- 1/4 cup chopped peanuts, for garnish
- Optional garnishes: chopped cilantro, sliced red chili, lime wedges

Instructions:

1. Cook the Noodles: Cook the spaghetti or noodles according to the package instructions until al dente. Drain and set aside.
2. Make the Sauce: In a medium bowl, whisk together the creamy peanut butter, soy sauce, rice vinegar, sesame oil, Sriracha sauce, minced garlic, grated ginger, honey or maple syrup, lime juice, and water until smooth. Add more water as needed to reach your desired consistency for the sauce.
3. Combine Noodles and Sauce: In a large mixing bowl, toss the cooked noodles with the prepared peanut sauce until the noodles are evenly coated.
4. Add Garnishes: Add the thinly sliced green onions to the noodles and toss to combine.
5. Serve: Divide the spicy peanut butter noodles into serving bowls. Garnish with chopped peanuts, chopped cilantro, sliced red chili, and lime wedges, if desired.
6. Enjoy! Serve the spicy peanut butter noodles immediately as a delicious and flavorful meal. They can be served warm or cold, making them perfect for meal prep or enjoying leftovers. Adjust the level of spiciness by adding more or less Sriracha sauce according to your taste preferences.

www.ingramcontent.com/pod-product-compliance
Lightning Source LLC
LaVergne TN
LVHW081615060526
838201LV00054B/2269